In the COMPANY OF ANGELS

Diane L. O'Brien

ISBN 979-8-88644-999-0 (Paperback)
ISBN 979-8-88851-000-1 (Digital)

Covenant Books
11661 Hwy 707
Murrells Inlet, SC 29576
www.covenantbooks.com

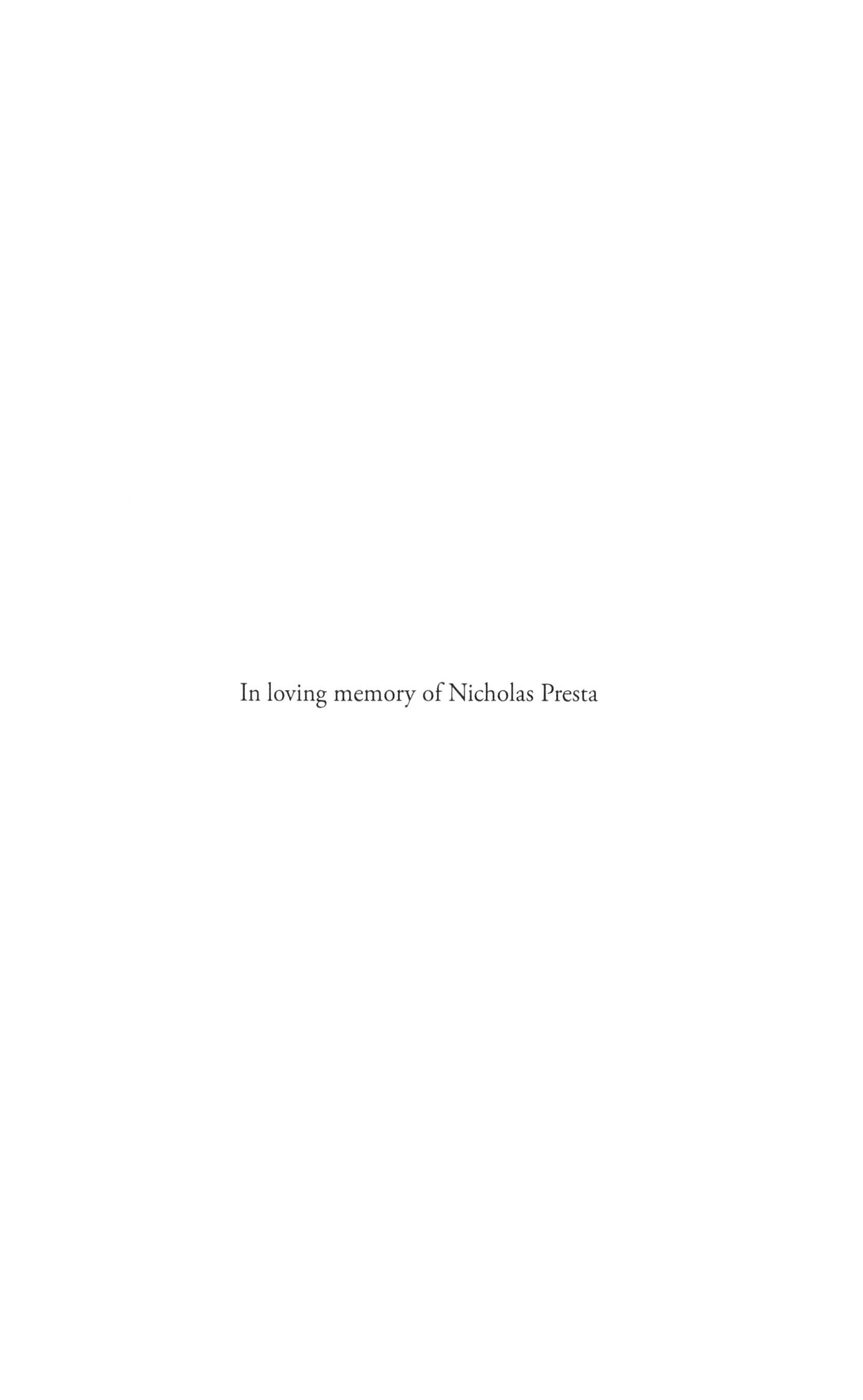
In loving memory of Nicholas Presta

Acknowledgments

I'm forever grateful to my husband, Mike, who supported my goal of establishing a nonprofit from our garage to moving to each warehouse and the trials along the way. Thanks to Jacob and Makena for your love and support. To my mother, Alma, who has always been there for me, always willing to lend a hand at home or in the warehouse. My sister, Laura, my best friend, thank you. To Aunt Mary, Amee, Sam, Jackie, Antonio, Sammy, Jessica, Joey, Devin, and Leo, you are so special. I am so fortunate to be able to count on your help. I love you all.

My volunteers, Kathy, Mickey (a.k.a. Sarge), Ray, Joy, Judy, Dave, Brenda, Joey, Diane, Terry, Sharon, Mike, Karen, Sandy, Sarah, Vicki, Barb, and Leslie, thank you all. You are the best!

—Michelle

Prologue

June 24, 1981

The Virgin Mary appeared to six children in Medjugorje, a town in Bosnia and Herzegovina.

This is a true story of one woman's destined search to understand life, but instead found God and a life-altering faith. Her name is Michelle Maxia.

Chapter 1

FAMILY TREE

> Freedom to dig the common earth, to drink the
> universal air, for this they sought refuge o'er wave and
> continent to link Egypt with Texas in their mystic
> chain and truth's perpetual lamp forbid to wane.
> —Emma Lazarus, *Selected Poems
> and Other Writings*

Imagine leaving your homeland and your siblings with nothing but memories and a determination to provide a better life for your family. Imagine fleeing with your wife and baby girl from the Russian occupation of Lithuania. Imagine your fear and the panic when the train carrying you to freedom was hit by a bomb and you walked the rest of the way on foot into an unknown city.

The year was 1944, and the displaced person camp was in Wurzburg, West Germany. Michelle Maxia's mother, Alma, was two years old.

Wurzburg was one of the largest camps, with populations varying from 2,500 to 5,500. The camp was divided into sections. Shel's grandparents, Emma and Peter, were in the American section. DPs, as they were called, were given food, which was rationed, clothing, and medical care, in addition to shelter. The camp was comprised of craftsmen, musicians, artists, and teachers. By 1945, newsletters, magazines, and newspapers were published. Wurzburg is one of the

1

locations in Germany which established a school for adult education called a folk school. Secondary schools or gymnasium schools and primary schools were opened.

In 1947, Emma and Peter added to their family with the arrival of a baby girl they named Mary. Peter and Emma did not know where they would be sent, as Peter's letters to a cousin in Chicago asking him to sponsor them went unanswered. Between 1947 and 1953, over 170,000 displaced persons were sent to Australia. The day before Peter and Emma were to depart, a letter from Chicago arrived. Their cousin agreed to sponsor them!

Tears were streaming down their faces as Emma, holding Mary, and Pete, holding Alma, gazed at Ellis Island. As the Statue of Liberty came into view, they were filled with joy and reverence. Lady Liberty's outstretched arm extended a welcome, her beacon a symbol of freedom. The year was 1950. Alma was seven, and Mary was two.

Michelle's grandparents worked tirelessly and although poor, saved for a home with every paycheck. Pete and Emma both found work at the Chicago stockyards. Pete went on to work at Hotpoint. Emma retired from Cherry Brand Meat Company. Alma and Mary witnessed how hard their parents worked, always dreaming of owning their own home.

Their dream came true. Peter and Emma bought an apartment building which housed four apartments. They maintained all four apartments and cut the grass with a push mower. The building was located on a corner. In later years, Shel, her sister Laura, and their cousin's chore was to cut the grass, a lot of grass! Alma and Mary watched their parents build a life for them, working all their lives, giving the girls a stable home, teaching them to recycle to make do. The girls grew to be strong and independent. They married, each taking an apartment in their parents' building. They were a close-knit family surrounded by love. When grandchildren came along, the cousins were like sisters and brothers nurtured in a home with a strong foundation that was instilled at an early age with perseverance. Alma is Michelle's mother.

Michelle relates, "My mother gained her strength from my grandparents. She never gave up, returning to school later in life to receive a nursing degree. My aunt Mary is also a nurse, both strong women. My grandma taught us to be frugal. She would pick up articles in the street, bring them home, and wash them. My grandparents worked ten- to twelve-hour days, always striving. My mother passed her never-give-up determination to me and gave me the gift of perseverance. I owe her so much. Thanks, Mom, for always being there."

Mary Emma Alma Peter
Photo taken in Wurzburg, West Germany.

Chapter 2

SHOOTING HOOPS

Michelle found solace in sports from the age of five. Raised by a single mother, she loved that it took her mind away from an absentee father, and she sought the company of other kids either on the court or baseball field. It helped ease the pain and sadness.

In high school Shel, like so many teens, tried alcohol. Beers after a game went down too easy. Shel remembers, "As I got older, I went on a bit of a wild path." She sought help for alcohol addiction at the age of twenty-three. "I met Bill Wilson, who became a good friend. Bill introduced me to an amazing group of people who have stayed with me. Meeting Bill and his friends was the first game changer in my spiritual life."

Working at Midway Airlines as a baggage handler gave her time to reflect on past events, and spiritual confusion became a recurring companion. A friend introduced her to Father Brankin, who convinced Shel she should get counseling. His parish, Saint Rosa Lima, was in Chicago, in a neighborhood fraught with poverty and gangs.

Father Pat endured a barrage of questions and sarcasm during the initial meeting and others. Shel was not Catholic, went to church on Easter and Christmas, and unloaded on the poor man. Years of poor choices bubbled to the surface.

A friendship developed. Shel was warming to Father Pat and was surprised to actually look forward to their meetings. Father Pat asked her to help keep kids off the street by coaching basketball.

Little did she know, the day she walked into that church basement, she would embark on a path she now realizes was divine intervention. Weeks went by, and the kids' "tough guy" exterior melted away; as did Shel's. She loved these kids; the world outside could be forgotten.

Sometime later, a friend mentioned Medjugorje, explaining it was a place in Bosnia and Herzegovina where people of every faith pilgrimage to visit the site where the Virgin Mary appeared in 1981. Her friend's account went in one ear and out the other. Shel was working at Midway and planning to buy a car while playing basketball at Saint Rosa Lima and enjoying hanging out with her friends in her free time.

The first sign occurred while she was walking through the airport—a newspaper left on a seat opened to an article.

Huh, it's that place, Medjugorje. Wow, people do believe this is the place the Virgin Mary appeared to six kid s, Michelle thought.

The second sign days later, a book, again on a seat, written about Medjugorje, by Wayne Weibel, who was also a Lutheran like Shel.

The third sign came the next payday. Shel was in the Midway Airlines' office to purchase a ticket to Florida to visit a friend. On the wall was a poster. Shel stared in disbelief. The cost to fly to Yugoslavia was only $16, which was the tax.

Shel thought, *Wow, this is really getting creepy.*

Searching open weeks to fly standby, there was one week available in June. Shel bought the ticket, as it was the final day to purchase, then went to the vacation department to try and get that week in June approved. The woman there unfortunately said that that week was booked. Shel walked out of her office feeling she tried. Her going to Medjugorje wasn't in the cards.

Walking down the street, Shel heard her name and turned to see the woman from the vacation department waving her arm.

"You won't believe this," she said. "As soon as you left, the phone rang. Someone canceled the week you want."

Shel accepted the open slot.

She left the office swearing and mentally kicking herself in her butt for buying a ticket to a place no one ever heard of, in the middle of nowhere, without money. "How stupid! I'll have to sell my car," Shel murmured to herself.

A voice broke through her rants, "Just come."

"Oh shit," Shel said. "I'm delusional. My brain is fried. I'm hearing things."

Another voice broke in, a coworker's. "Shel, Shel, are you okay? You're in the middle of the street!"

Shel bought the ticket May 2. Years later, her son, Jacob, was born that day and later, a daughter, Makena, also on May 2.

One week later, back at Saint Rosa Lima, Father Pat was delighted. "Surely," he said, "your entire life is about to change."

Shel told him, "Simmer down, Padre. Bring it down a notch. I'm just going to check out what's going on there."

Not long after, Shel was called to the church from the basement. Michelle recalls, "In the middle of my time with the kids, I was called to go and see Father Pat. Exasperated, swearing, and sweating profusely, I entered the church. Smiling faces turned to look at me. What was going on?"

Father Pat presented Shel with an envelope. It seemed the parishioners had collected money for her trip.

"No, Father. I won't take this," she said.

His reply interrupted her, "These people gave you this money in faith. You need to take it in faith."

While driving home, Shel was so overwhelmed and in awe thinking how those kind, gracious people who lived in a poor community would give her money. One last obstacle stood in her way. Shel needed a passport.

"Aha," she said. "Here's a test. If the passport arrives on time, I'm going. If not, oh well."

The passport came. God had begun to reveal Himself. Shel relates, "I didn't realize it then." Reluctant and scared to be going alone, Shel thought she would go to Medjugorje and return to her carefree, fun-loving life. Nothing could be further from the truth.

Chapter 3

INCREDULOUS JOURNEY

June 1990

While on the flight to Bosnia and Herzegovina, Shel met a tour group from Illinois. They fortunately were on the same flight home and invited her to join them on the bus back to the airport. Shel didn't feel quite so alone. She boarded the first of three buses to Medjugorje with chickens as traveling companions.

The last bus stopped in front of Saint James Church. A villager had a vision to build a church large enough to accommodate thousands, although only about two hundred parishioners attended mass in 1925 when construction plans were made. Ten years later, in 1935, the building began. The church was completed in 1969. When Shel was there, the church was filled to overflowing. Crowds today number three times the capacity. Shel walked through town but found no hotels or restaurants. Finally, coming to some confessionals in front of the church, Shel approached one with a sign that said, "English."

The priest said, "Come in, my child."

Shel said, "Can you come out? I'm not Catholic."

The priest was from a tour group from Colorado, and he took her to the home where they were staying. A little old lady with a babushka on her head said she had one room left, and it came with two meals a day. Shel asked, "How much?"

"Twenty dollars."

"That I could pay."

7

Chapter 4

MOUNT KRIŽEVAC AND APPARITION HILL

Križevac is the highest mountain in Medjugorje. In 1933, the 1900th anniversary of Christ's death, the local parishioners of Saint James erected a concrete cross on this hill, carrying materials up the rock-strewn slope. The cross was completed on March 15, 1934.

> Dear children, the cross was also in God's plan when you built it. These days especially, go on the mountain and pray before the cross. I need your prayers. Thank you for having responded to my call. (Our Lady, August 30, 1984)

The first night, Shel, tired from the long trip, just wanted to go to bed, yet was drawn to Cross Hill. The reason was unclear, but she felt she had to go there.

"This is insane, totally nuts. What is wrong with me climbing up here to babysit rocks? Great, just great."

Later, Shel was told by villagers that there was always someone who spends the night on Cross Hill, always. Shel thought, *Why me?*

Apparition Hill began as a pile of rocks and became a statue made by an Italian sculptor. Our Lady appeared there on June 25, 1981, and many times since. The Virgin Mary appeared to six children, ages 10 to 17, on June 24, 1981. They are Mirjana Dragicevic, Ivanka Ivankovic, Marija Pavlovic, Jakov Colo, Vicka Ivankovic, and Ivan Dragicevic. Our Lady still appears today to three of these visionaries. People of all faiths pilgrimage to Medjugorje yearly.

That night, Shel went up Apparition Hill with the Colorado group. Every Friday, Shel learned Vicka would come to Apparition Hill, where she would experience her daily apparition. She would then share the message that evening. Shel learned that after Vicka receives the apparition, a phenomenon would always occur.

Michelle was looking at Mount Križevac when she heard the crowd behind her gasp. As she turned, someone from the Colorado group said, "Did you see that?"

Shel replied, "See what?"

They said, "A star in the sky was spinning and then took off."

The crowd gasped again, and again the Colorado group looked stunned and said, "Did you see that?"

Shel said, "See what?"

One of the group members explained, "Three clouds came together."

Shel said, "No, I didn't see that."

What Shel did see the second time was an explosion of light, then three white lights appeared, moving at first in a circular motion, then at an angle. As the lights continued to turn, they turned into three red crosses. Shel thought of the crown of thorns in that moment. Then two white lights appeared, which Shel thought looked like eyes. After they disappeared, one white light followed and blinked three times. Shel turned to the Colorado group and said, "Did you see that?"

They said, "No."

The next morning, Shel mentioned the lights she saw the evening before.

"Michelle, there aren't any lights around the Cross," they responded.

Shel, knowing what she saw, replied, "Yes, there are. I saw them."

This time in unison, the others said, "No, there aren't."

Not to be put off, Shel was determined to prove them wrong. She trudged up Mount Križevac, combing every rock for the lights and wiring. Much to her amazement, there were no lights.

About 6:30 p.m., another strange phenomenon took place, but this time, others saw it too. It is called the Miracle of the Sun, first witnessed in Portugal near Fatima in 1917. Shel saw something spinning in the air, like a disk.

"Wow," she said, "there's that Miracle of the Sun thing going on. Pretty wild. People worldwide have seen this mystery. What causes the sun to look as if its spinning? Then there are the lights on the hill. I know they were there."

Later, Father Jozo was giving people His blessing, and Shel joined the Colorado group. When Father Jozo approached her, he didn't bless her head. He blessed her eyes. Shel clutched his arm and said, "Why did you do that? Am I going to go blind?"

Father Jozo replied, "No, the Holy Spirit guides me."

The next day, Shel followed the Colorado group who were going to see Father Peter Mary Rookey (1916–2014). Father Rookey wrote the Miracle Prayer.

Shel relates, "I sat in the bleachers and watched as Father Peter laid his hands on people who would fall back into waiting arms. I thought that was a bit much. Then an Irish young man about sixteen went down, and his body started to tremble. He spread his arms and then placed his hands on his chest. He opened his eyes and spoke to his dad, who was with him, that he saw the Virgin Mary. He asked Our Lady to speak through him, and she replied, 'It's not your path.'"

On Shel's last day in Medjugorje, she was told the faithful would light a candle in appreciation at each hill. She recalls, "On my way to get candles, I saw that Father Rookey was at it again. This time, I decided to come off the bleachers and into the arena and be open to the experience. When it was my turn, I found myself on the ground, and my whole body was tingling from the inside out. I got up and thought to myself that that was pretty cool. I bought the candles and went to Mount Križevac first, thinking I couldn't leave the candles at the bottom. So I climbed up to the top. I got to the top and was alone, thinking the entire time, *Why was I called there?*

"A man knelt within three feet of me. He said that he was from Switzerland and had arrived the night I'd seen the lights on Apparition Hill. He told me he was on Mount Križevac at the time everyone else was on Apparition Hill. He had pitched his tent behind the Cross. I asked him if he saw lights. He replied no, but he was very cold in his tent and prayed for warmth. In that moment, he felt an explosion of heat. I told him I looked for wires, and he laughed.

"On the way down Mount Križevac, I felt an overwhelming truth that God loved me. I thought, *What are the odds I would be the only person in a village of thousands to witness the lights?* I apologized for doubting His involvement in my life. I cried, racked with tears from the deepest part of my soul.

"I headed for Apparition Hill. It was dark, and while I was sitting there, I saw a young man sitting with a friend. It was the Irish boy that went down with Father Rookey earlier. All of a sudden, he went down and started trembling. His friend looked at me and said, 'Help.' Going over to her, I said, 'He's going to be okay. Let's sit here and wait.' The man spread his arms out, smiled, stopped trembling, and looked at me and said, 'Mary blesses you.' I said, 'You can't tell people things. You're not one of the visionaries!' He then asked why I was there and said, 'What just happened was for you.'"

Shel walked down Apparition Hill, saying, "Why me? What is going on?"

At once came a voice, "Why not you?"

Shel knew she had to return and tell people that Medjugorje was real.

Shel remembered Father Jozo had blessed her eyes. Shel came to realize it was God's way of opening her eyes and her heart. She felt that Mary called her to Medjugorje and called her to her Son.

Shel's mom and sister were waiting at the airport. When she approached, they looked at her and started to cry. The pupils of her eyes were in the shape of crosses.

Father Pat, back at Saint Rosa Lima, was delighted with Shel's account of her trip.

"Medjugorje did for you what would take me a lifetime to do."

Michelle lightly punched his arm. "Thanks a lot, wise guy." Shel returned with rosaries and medals for the parishioners in appreciation for their faith in her.

Shel felt a relationship with God from that time on. In retrospect, she came to realize He would shine through her, and she became a conduit. Years since have proven she is just that. We now know Shel has a "direct line," and time and time again she has witnessed everyday miracles too numerous to mention.

She found that stopping at church most mornings brought about a peacefulness. Fifteen minutes sitting in solitude with God became as needed as her morning coffee. She relied on both.

Talking with coworkers about Medjugorje kept memories alive. Shel's enthusiasm was contagious, and a group planned for a trip there the following June. Unfortunately, the Croatian War of Independence had begun in 1991. Everyone but Shel's friend Dan decided to cancel.

They embarked one year after her first trip. Shel was confident this journey would be different. She knew the ropes.

Flying standby, they were jolted from their slumber to hear the pilot announce that the airplane was not allowed to land in Bosnia. He flatly stated that the airline hadn't paid its usage fees. They were being diverted to Zagreb, the capitol of Croatia. Shel looked at Dan, who appeared white as a ghost.

"Oh no," he said.

Shel replied, "Oh shit, I wish I had studied the language!" They were over an hour from Medjugorje and flying standby, landing in a country at war. There were not any buses going to Medjugorje. The flight attendant told them to go see Dooshka at the welcome booth; he could help them.

Michelle remembers, "We see this guy in suspenders in the airport at a welcome desk, sweating and holding a cigarette with two inches of ash. He was smiling at us. Thankfully he spoke English. We explained that we were trying to get to Medjugorje. He looked at me, then at Dan, and said, 'I like you, but I can't help you. You go now.'"

Hungry and cold, Shel and Dan left the airport and walked to the town, where they found an open restaurant and inquired,

"English?" The waiter gazed around and asked if anyone spoke English. No one did. Desperate times called for desperate measures. Dan began mooing, and Michelle clucked and waved her arms like she was doing the chicken dance. They ate chicken legs washed down with milk!

They walked back to the airport, but security told them they could not sleep there. Shel and Dan were sitting on a bench when a young man approached. He spoke English and offered to call his dad, who might know where they could stay. The dad and he talked to a friend who agreed to let them spend the night. He said, "My dad is coming to pick you up."

Waiting outside the airport, Shel was reminded of a scene in a movie. A man sped around the curve in a little Fiat.

"We piled in and headed down dark roads," Shel recalled. "We should have begged to be allowed to stay in the airport. This wasn't a good idea."

They arrived at a house, and a little old lady came to the door. She led them up a long flight of stairs to a small room with one narrow bed and a sink. Dan, ever the gentleman, said, "Shel, you take the bed. I'll sleep on the floor."

Shel replied, "The floor is cement. It's freezing. You can't sleep on the floor."

Dan crawled on top of the covers, Shel under them. She could feel his body shivering next to hers.

"Dan," she said, "listen to me, you need to get under the covers. This is survival."

Dan welcomed the heat from Shel's body and felt the warmth from head to toe. It was a long night.

Not getting much sleep, they heard a knock early the next morning. The little old lady was at the door holding a tray with coffee, bagels, and jelly. The Fiat came and drove them back to the airport. Neither their host nor driver would accept payment.

Tours were canceled that year due to the war, so Shel and Dan didn't have long to wait before they boarded a plane to take them to Bosnia, where they boarded a bus to Medjugorje. They found the town empty. Shel knocked on the door of the same house she stayed in the year before. A young girl who spoke English answered, and she said, "Yes, we have two rooms available at the same rate as last year."

Shel asked if there would be a message from Apparition Hill that evening.

"Yes," the girl's mother replied, "Jakov, the youngest visionary, is giving the message."

Later, Shel and Dan climbed Apparition Hill. Shel asked a girl next to them what time Jakov would be here. The girl replied, "Jakov is sitting next to you."

Jakov looked at Shel, who smiled and gave him the "Hi, what's up?" nod and excitedly turned to Dan. "Dan, that's him, Jakov. He's next to me!"

Within fifteen minutes, a throng of people were gathered on Apparition Hill. Everyone knelt. Shel, so close to Jakov she could have touched him, inched closer, hoping Mary could see her too! Jakov stood and spoke loudly, sharing our Lady's message.

"Dear children, today on this great day which you have given to me, I desire to bless all of you and to say these days while I am with you are days of grace. I desire to teach you and help you to walk the way of holiness. There are many people who do not desire to understand my messages and to accept with seriousness what I am saying. But you I therefore call and ask that, by your lives and by your daily living, you witness my presence. If you pray, God will help you to discover the true reason for my coming. Therefore, little children, pray and read the Sacred Scriptures so that through my coming, you discover the message in Sacred Scripture for you. Thank you for having responded to my call" (June 25, 1991).

After Shel returned from Medjugorje, she gave all her medals and rosaries away. A woman she knew was going there, and Shel asked her to bring her fifty medals. Two months passed. Shel was walking a customer in a wheelchair to her gate when the woman noticed Shel's medal on her keychain. Shel remembers the woman saying, "Oh, your medal, that is from Medjugorje. I've always wanted to go there, but now my health is so bad I'll never go. It's the one thing I wanted to do."

At once Shel heard a voice, "Give her the medal."

Shel was human and argued with the voice, "But it's my last medal! I'm not surrendering right away." She got in a debate with the voice.

The voice continued, "You have been there. You don't need a medal."

Michelle begrudgingly gave the woman her medal. The woman, holding it to her cheek, said, "Thank you," and started to cry.

Shel said, "There are blessings attached to that medal. Don't ever stop praying."

The woman replied, "I never will."

Shel watched the plane pull away from the gate, realizing she would never see her medal again. She turned when a woman walked up to her and said, "Close your eyes and hold up your hand."

Shel recognized she was the woman who told her some time ago that she was going to Medjugorje. Feeling something cold, Shel opened her eyes and started to get teary.

"What's the matter?" the woman said. "You asked me to get them, fifty medals."

"Don't you understand? I just gave a woman on that plane my last medal." Shel was so glad she listened to that voice.

Shel with soldiers in Zagreb.

Shel with her hosts in Medjugorje.

Shel's host home.

Shel's host heating the stove for dinner.

Shel serenading the goats on Apparition Hill.

Shel and Dan went up the hill to fetch a pail of water. Dan fell down, nearly broke his crown, the fellow was feelin' quite mellow.

Shel Cross Hill

Views from Cross Hill.

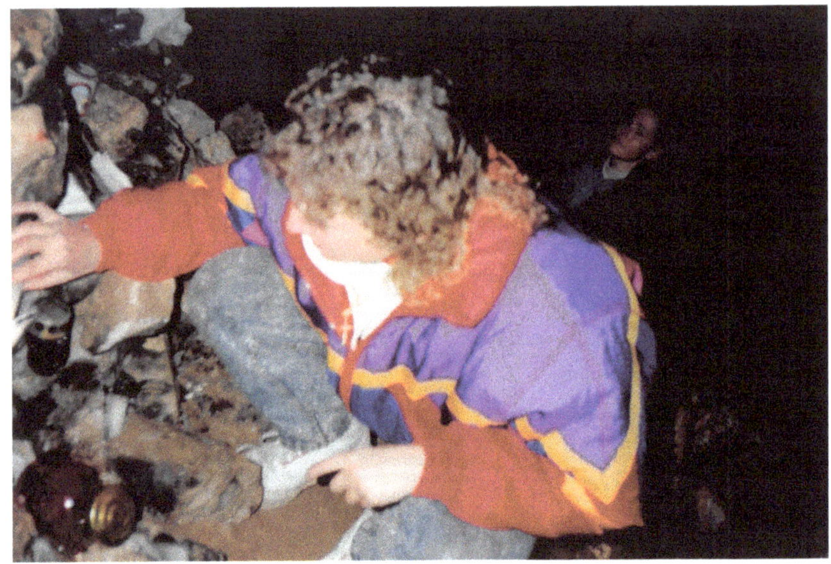

Shel lighting a candle on Apparition Hill.

St James Church

Chapter 5

CHANCE ENCOUNTER

In the weeks following Shel's trip to Medjugorje, she began reading the Bible. Not beginning to end, since in her words, "That's not how I roll," but randomly opening to a passage. Shel was still stopping in church most days but was not ready to embrace Catholicism.

One night, Shel had a dream. Hands were above her head, water pouring down on her. The next day, the Bible passage read, "From me will come living waters." Soon after, while sitting in church, Shel prayed, "God, I'm ready to meet someone."

Mike Maxia was born in Kansas City, Kansas, the youngest of six. His father relocated the family to Wisconsin believing they could become farmers. That did not happen. His father started a food distribution business, and Mike worked for him during high school. When Mike was seventeen, he lost his best friend, his brother, in a tragic accident. He was nineteen. The brothers were so close, the sudden emptiness Mike felt over losing him filled him with grief. Mike's dad died two years later. Mike eventually started his own food distribution business. He was at Midway Airport on his way to Texas to visit his godfather when he crossed paths with Shel. It was August 1991.

"I heard her before I saw her, laughing with her coworkers at the gate. She was animated, and I was drawn to her. Wanting to get closer, I decided to ask about my flight delay."

"What's going on with all these flights?" Mike asked.

Shel looked into smiling warm eyes intent on her face.

"God's in charge of this one," she replied.

Mike asked, "Are you religious?"

"No," Shel said, "I'm spiritual. Religion is just a bunch of rules."

Walking away from the counter to some seats nearby, Mike thoughtfully said, "Everybody needs rules, but do you know God's will?"

Shel and Mike talked for an hour. The fog was clearing, and they heard Mike's flight announced. Mike said, "Would you like to continue this conversation when I come back from my trip?"

Shel decided to give him her number, although he offered his first, in case she was reluctant to give him personal information. She was attracted to Mike and felt the feeling was mutual. She liked his low-key demeanor, his eyes meeting hers, and he listened. The conversation flowed.

Later that day, Shel mentioned meeting Mike to her girlfriend, who stated, "You're going to marry that guy!"

Shel remembered her prayer that morning. She had prayed to meet someone. She was to discover Mike had also prayed someone would come into his life.

Mike came back early from Texas, explaining to his godfather that he met someone at the airport, someone special. He nervously called and asked Shel out to dinner. Shel was dogsitting for her aunt who was on vacation. She invited him over to her aunt's house to watch a movie. He brought Chinese food, and they talked about music. Shel loved rock and roll; Mike liked Yanni. Mike preferred cold weather; Shel liked it hot. They found they both loved sports, and both were very competitive. When it was time to eat, Mike asked if he could say a prayer.

Wow, thought Shel, and her attraction grew.

Engrossed in one another, neither remembered much of the movie. Mike gently kissed Shel good night, leaving her wanting more. Shel realized she finally found a man who was on the same page and was anxious to see Mike again. Shel did see Mike again, every day for the next three years!

Shel, reflecting on those years, explains their relationship ran on constant energy. They competed in cards, darts, shooting pool, bowling, playing tennis, and every game. They both loved to travel. Shel loves telling the story about their trip to Wyoming to visit Mike's sister. Mike tried to win a stuffed animal at a carnival, throwing a baseball at a target. Shel asked Mike to let her try. All those years playing ball came in handy. Shel won a stuffed animal on the first try and gave it to Mike!

Mike and Shel loved to ski, but Mike excelled skiing downhill backward! Shel was really impressed; no way would she attempt that. Mike was amazing on skis. Shel found Mike amazing, period.

Mike encouraged Shel to continue meeting with Father Pat, who was transferred from Saint Rosa Lima, then transferred again to Gurnee, Illinois. Shel drove there for religious classes until Father Pat was transferred to Oklahoma, where he was given the title of monsignor. Shel flew to Oklahoma for her confirmation into the Catholic faith. Mike proposed, confident he had found his soulmate.

Father Pat flew to Chicago to marry Shel and Mike on a blistering hot day in July 1995. Shel loves Father Pat and as he was instrumental in her faith journey, was grateful to him on many levels.

"There we were, facing one another in front of God and everyone, when I felt dizzy, wiping sweat from my face," Shel said. "My sister noticed and thought it was due to being unused to makeup. I went down. My sister reached out to soften my fall. I came to staring into Mike's alarmed face. He thought I had died. 'It's all your fault, Padre. Your homily was way too long,' I said jokingly. I was wiping Mike's forehead. Father Pat looked at Mike and said, 'Mike, you will never get the last word.'"

Shel and Mike had their honeymoon in Makena, a quiet area on Maui. They found a home in each other's arms and an awareness they were meant to meet that foggy day at Midway.

Michelle and Mike
July 1995
Hawaii

Chapter 6

TO PROTECT AND SERVE

Midway Airlines dissolved on November 13, 1991. Shel stood in the unemployment line on her birthday, thinking this wasn't supposed to be happening. Mike offered her a job with his company, which was located on Thirty-First Street in Chicago. Shel's desk faced a window, and one day, she saw two guys beating another guy on the street, one picking up a brick. Shel sprang from her chair, ran to them, yelling, "Stop, police!" They ran. She only later realized that that wasn't smart since she didn't carry a gun or wear a badge. She also realized that the young man on the ground could have died from being hit on the head with a brick. Shel's dad and cousin were police officers. She never hesitated running toward danger. Maybe she could apply to the force and possibly make a difference. Shel applied with the sheriff's department, passed the test, and was waiting to be called. After one year, she was accepted to the police academy and loved every minute of her time there.

In January 1992, Shel started at the academy. She related this incident, "So when we were at the academy, I earned a marksman pin. Funny story. The guy next to me and I were shooting at the range when we were tested. The lights went on, and the instructor pulled our targets forward and then asked me to take my weapon out of the holster and open it to see if I had any bullets left. He asked me how many bullets my gun held. He then counted the holes on my target and asked me where I got the extra bullet. I looked at him, perplexed, until he asked the guy next to me to open his weapon and then asked him where his extra bullet was because he was one hole short on his target! When the target pulled up, I was really aggravated. Every shot was in the center except for one hole in the top right corner. I couldn't believe that happened. My instructor looked at me and said, 'Well, we definitely have a certified markswoman in our presence.'

"When we started at the academy, they advised not to practice on your own if you have never shot a gun before, and wait until we go through our first instruction and we will learn everything we need to know to be a great shot. We don't want to learn bad habits." Shel waited.

"I listened and waited for our first instruction. I was a good athlete, always good at basketball and softball. I knew I had a good eye and good coordination. I waited for instructions and boy oh boy, I took off like nobody's business."

Shel became the second woman in Illinois to teach defense tactics and physical skills in the sheriff's academy. In August of that year, Shel became pregnant. Motherhood beckoned.

Shel was transferred to the courthouse in Bridgeview on April 1997, guarding the back doors in the basement.

Shel fondly recalls, "My grandma actually took two sheriff shirts and sewed them together to make a maternity top. By the time March came, I could no longer wear my gun belt—it wouldn't fit! I felt like the pregnant sheriff in the movie *Fargo*!"

Shel left the sheriff's department in April, one month before their son, Jacob, was born on May 2, 1997. She wanted to be a stay-at-home mother. May 2 was the same day she had bought her ticket to Medjugorje. "I went from shopping at Macy's to Target, but found great bargains at garage sales. Jacob and I would drive to the neighborhoods, and it wasn't long before I hated paying full price for anything."

Looking back, several events remain in Shel's memory while on the police force, one woman's story in particular.

"A woman was sitting in the lockup crying. I walked over to her, and through tears, she claimed she was innocent, which they all say. I looked at her report, and at that time when picked up on a warrant, there was no picture and no bond. I contacted the Chicago police officer who issued the warrant and asked if he could come to the lockup. I asked if he remembered the case, and he did, then asked if he would come back to the cell. The officer did and said that this was not her and that we arrested the wrong person."

Shel was on very good terms with the judge and walked to his office with the officer who explained, "Judge, you have the wrong woman."

The judge said, "Call the prosecutor right now."

To the officer he said, "You stay here. Mom's going home today."

Shel walked back to the cell and said, "Think you're going home today."

The woman began to cry, taking Shel's hand. She thought she would be held over the holidays, but now would be home for Christmas. Shel was later to learn the woman's cousin had used her information, and that was how the police thought they had the right woman. Shel brought the woman before the judge, and he immediately released her. The woman's eldest daughter came to pick her up. Shel had learned that their electricity had been turned off. There wasn't money for food or gifts. Her daughter was in college, and Mom was alone, raising her family.

Shel and her partner, Tony, collected gift cards, clothes, food, and gifts for the family. The judge, prosecutor, and their coworkers at the sheriff's department came together. They had the electricity on the next day.

Tony's truck was filled when they drove to Roseland, an area on Chicago's south side, to deliver Christmas to the family.

"Tony and I drove into Roseland, not a good part of town, holding our badges in the air. We knocked on her door. A child answered and said that his mom wasn't home."

"Tell your mom it's Officer Michelle," Shel told the child.

The mom came to the door explaining that she was terrified she was being picked up again. She stood in overwhelming joy as we unloaded food, clothes, and gifts of toys. The family laughed and danced around the living room.

Shel said, "We want you to know we care. All of us. The prosecutor, judge, and department care. This is the least we could do." Turning to the daughter, Shel smiled and said, "You finish college. Your siblings will follow you. Be the leader."

A fire was lit. It felt so good to help people with their lives. The fire ignited that cold Christmas, and it continues to burn today. Shel was unaware that thousands of children and adults would feel its warmth.

Chapter 7 begins with the early days of what would become the nonprofit Toybox Connection. In Shel's words, "God had a plan."

Chapter 7

WAREHOUSE WOES

Shel and Mike were blessed with a beautiful baby girl and again on May 2, in 2000. They named her Makena, after the town in Maui where their married life began.

"Prior to Makena's arrival, I started Toy Swap, an online toy exchange, which was a huge success. Toy Swap grew to thousands of hits a day. The website included a donation section, and people found a home for their gently used toys, which were distributed among nonprofits. The website crashed and burned, and I couldn't get it going," Shel relates. "I knew my time with toys was not over and felt God was calling me to create an entity that did not exist, collecting and distributing toys to those in need."

Shel received her 5013C classification and launched her non-profit on December 26, 2007. A plan materialized to find a space large enough to store donations and connect them to nonprofits. "Our first warehouse was fifteen hundred square feet, without a bathroom or office," Shel recalls. "We didn't have air-conditioning and little heat. Mike no longer had his own company, and although employed, we lived on much less. I funded everything we needed at the warehouse with my credit card. I believed in Toybox so much I felt it would be okay to do that. Mike supported me one hundred percent. We painted the floors and put in a drop ceiling. The following March, I took the kids from Mooseheart out for a day of fun."

Mooseheart is a home for boys and girls from birth through their teen years, thirty-eight miles west of Chicago. Established in 1913 on a one-thousand-acre campus, children attend school, compete in sports, and are provided a stable, nurturing environment. Moose Lodge members across the country pay dues, which supports the school. Every year since, excluding two years due to COVID, Shel plans a day of fun for the Mooseheart kids. A lunch is included and gifts for all.

My husband Terry and I met Shel in the parking lot outside of Warehouse One. We can't recall why we were in the area and certainly not why we stopped. If you know our boss, you know Shel is a talker and especially loves to talk about Toybox. We offered to pick donations up in our van—a mistake. Shel sent us fifty miles away, often for one bag!

Two years later, Shel moved to Warehouse Two, also without a bathroom, office, or heat. "My friend had a machine shop and had space in the back, about a thousand square feet," Shel said. "We had to pull pallets up on huge shelving units with a forklift. We continued operations there about a year. I wrapped Christmas presents for shoppers in the mall as a fundraiser, and the manager asked what I needed. I said I really need some warehouse space. She showed me Warehouse Three, our current location. When my only warehouse volunteer at the time, Kathy, walked in, she said, 'Oh my gosh, Shel, it's so big.' I told her, 'I have a feeling we're going to outgrow it!'"

Shel was right. Years later, she laughed when Kathy reminded her of that conversation.

"So the warehouse needed a lot of work, but I saw the potential," Shel recalls. "The mall management added double doors, but everything else was up to us. Mike and I spent an entire summer repairing walls. We rented a machine to pull up the carpeting, which had been glued to the cement floor. We scraped the glue and hired a company to wash the floor, clearing it of dust. No easy task. The warehouse is eight thousand square feet!

"As a police officer, I saw so many children with nothing. I knew I had the energy, ability, and willingness to change their situations. I wanted to bring joy to as many children as I could. I created a Sheriff's Day Out. We took a group from the Department of Children and Family Services to the Discovery Zone, which is a family-owned fun center. We bought them gifts and took them to McDonald's. Children need to know there are people who care.

"I have worked on my connection with God, growing it every day. I focus on God's will for me. Believe me, He made it very clear that my talent wasn't singing or dancing, so I focused on the gifts I believed I was good at, and communication was key. Making people smile and laugh comes naturally. Toybox has not been difficult when the mission is to help a child. I love the saying that came to me a long time ago. Together we are a moving force of goodness in the world.

"God knew what He was doing when He sent toys my way. I love to play with them. I love throwing balls at my volunteers. Give me a lightsaber and I'm Luke Skywalker."

Shel is a practical joker. She excels at her little tricks, and it makes her day to hear one of us scream when a lifelike snake is in our lunchbox! She especially loves spiders (the real scary ones) and delights in placing them on the toilet or floor in the bathroom. She relates the story of placing a realistic mouse in the cylinder at the drive-through at her bank. Howling with glee, she watched as the young teller screamed, paper flying. The time she planted her little mouse pal at the Midway Airlines ticket counter, the news spread through the airport.

"Shel's at it again!" they said.

Shel is always on the lookout for prank opportunities. Her cousin recently discovered a bat in her house, creating quite a stir. It was hanging from the bathroom shower rod. The dog was growling and barking, alerting everyone of their nighttime visitor. Finally caught with a fishing net, they were able to get back to bed. Shel, hearing of the story, bought some fake but very lifelike bats. Soon after, she received the expected call from her cousin shrieking, "You're hysterical!" into the phone. Seems she pulled back the covers on her bed to see the sheet covered with bats! Success!

Shel relates her antics with glee, stating, "If there is a purgatory for pranksters, I'll never get out!" She credits her paternal grandfather for giving her the "prankster gene," and their mutual love for the Three Stooges! "Why, certainly!"

Chapter 8, titled "Looney Toons," begins with the true story of how a young man's hobby became his profession. I'll also relate more incredible stories of what we at Toybox refer to as "Shel's direct line to our Lord."

Grandpa Charlie, prankster extraordinaire
Laura and Michelle

Michelle Jacob Makena Mike

C h a p t e r 8

LOONEY TUNES

While working with Mike on Warehouse Three, Shel looked around at the bare walls. A thought leaped into her mind. She remembered a young man she met when she was a police officer. He was doing some artwork for Home Depot at that time and attended classes at a community college. Shel decided to drive to Chicago to try and find him, which fortunately she did. His name is Christian.

"Hey, Christian," Shel said, "what's up? I would like you to do some painting for me."

Christian said, "Where?"

"In a warehouse in Orland Park," Shel explained.

Christian met Shel at the warehouse. Looking around at the walls, he asked, "What do you want me to paint?"

Shel said, "Cartoon characters, Christian, big ones, as many as you can fit."

Christian thought, "Okay, not hard."

Asking Shel which wall she wanted him to paint, he stared at her when she simply answered, "All of them."

When Christian began experimenting with art as a teenager, it was fun. "It's something that I always liked to do in my neighborhood when I was a kid," Christian said. "Some people think graffiti is art, and some people think it's rubbish. It's a hobby like anything else."

Dupont donated the spray paint cans, to Christian's delight. He brought the warehouse to life. Barney, Clifford the Dog, Lightning McQueen from the movie *Cars*, Elmo, SpongeBob SquarePants, and many others look down at us. Children and adults can't help but smile as they look at all their favorites.

Shel said, "How can you not walk in here and feel the joy? There's so much energy in all of the characters. It really represents who we are as a charity."

In April 2013, a local paper featured Christian on its front page titled, "The Art of the Matter." A half-page picture of Christian creating Elmo while Mickey Mouse, Bugs Bunny, and Goofy looked on captured a reader's attention. Impressed, he contacted the newspaper and explained he would like to meet the young man pictured on their front page. A meeting followed at the warehouse, but that's not all, folks! Our anonymous angel funded Christian through art school in Chicago!

When I began volunteering at Toybox, I didn't understand Shel's hesitation when she didn't unload items as soon as she could. The next situation explains why.

A basketball system was donated for outdoor use. Lots of eye-rolling was going on when Shel told us to store it in the back of the warehouse, which was already jammed. One year went by, two years passed, and in the third year, this is how the ball bounced. A teacher came in to pick up books and incentive items the kids buy with their "bonus bucks" for being stars in class. Shel asked if the school needed anything else. The woman hesitated, but said the Dad's Club really needed a basketball system. Shel began to laugh.

The woman looked at Shel and said, "Why are you laughing?"

Shel explained, "We've been holding on to one for you for over two years."

We haven't received another basketball system since. If this was an isolated case, I would dismiss the idea that Shel has a direct line. The truth is, we witness occurrences like this all the time. Shel confided she is in awe and feels the Holy Spirit is at work deep inside her. Shel feels her only job is to pay close attention."

It was the day before Christmas Eve. Shel received a call from Juan, who runs Alicia's House, the largest food pantry in Illinois. He had just received a call from the toy company that was to supply toys for a party he was having for the families he served. It seems the company was filing bankruptcy. Juan explained he was in dire need of toys, whatever Shel could spare. Shel asked, "How many toys do you need?"

Juan replied, "About five hundred."

Shel said, "Do you have a truck?"

Juan asked, "How many toys can you give us?"

Shel brought Juan to tears when she answered, "Five hundred. Juan, I'm not a cook, but I'm hosting Christmas. Cooking is a real challenge, so please be on time at the warehouse at 9:00 a.m."

Juan was waiting when Shel arrived and loaded five hundred gently used toys. He was ecstatic!

Juan called Shel after Christmas and said there was one toy on the table after the party, validating that every child received a toy. He has kept in touch over the years. His nonprofit has grown, and he is now opening an eleven-thousand-square-foot center for autistic children!

Juan said we saved Christmas for him that year. He was thrilled to receive the gently used toys, and at that time, in our first warehouse, that was all we had. Toybox Connection has grown. We now have new toys at Christmas, thanks to the generous friends we've come to know.

Another amazing Christmas story involved a request for gifts totaling sixty girls and seventy boys. We had a donation of exactly seventy miniature NASCARs for the boys but nothing suitable for the girls, who were older. Within the same day, the Girl Scouts arrived with sixty gift bags for girls. The bags included scarves and bath and body products, perfect for the age we needed. Shel jokes, "God knows I have a short-term memory, so He has to make things happen pretty quick!"

We received mattresses, large and small. When the twin mattresses came our way, let me tell you, we were not happy. "Where can we put all these mattresses?" we asked. As usual, we worried needlessly.

Our boss savors her family time. Her phone is constantly ringing at Toybox, and during the week, it's busy with people either dropping off donations or picking them up. A friend of hers asked if she would attend an information event for human-trafficking rescue. Shel told her friend, "Sorry, I can't go."

The woman persisted; it seemed a guest speaker was going to be in attendance. The speaker and her husband were opening a home for victims of sex trafficking. Shel finally relented and went with her friend to hear the speaker. After the service, Shel was introduced to the visitor and was very impressed with their home. "Well, we have bed frames. Our next fundraiser is for mattresses."

Shel laughed, looked at the woman, and simply said, "We have your mattresses! Spend the fundraising money on other needs."

Graco is well known for making baby furniture. Someone at their company saw Shel on WGN television and called to say that they would like to collect new toys for us. When she arrived with them, there were only forty toys, much to the kind woman's disappointment. She offered thirteen baby mattresses. Our eyes were rolling again; seems we were back in the mattress business.

Shel called Beacon Therapeutic Diagnostic and Treatment Center to tell them we had new baby toys for when they go into homes. Shel mentioned we also received thirteen baby mattresses.

"What did you just say?" the woman asked. "I just left a homeless shelter where there are thirteen babies without beds."

God knew who needed them. Thirteen babies slept in beds that night.

A woman called Shel to ask if we took baby things. She had a stroller, crib, changing table, and a highchair. Shel said sure. Before the woman was to come, Shel received another call from Kitty at the Family Enrichment Program, another nonprofit. A mom with a baby had a house fire. They were relocated, but all her baby things were lost in the fire. Kitty wondered if we had anything. Shel connected Kitty with the woman who called minutes earlier, giving her all the items she needed.

"God is at the helm," Shel said. "We just have to pay attention."

I'll close "Looney Toons" with one last heartwarming story that can only be described as magical.

Homewood Disposal Company arrived, towing a huge red sleigh filled with toys. Santa brought a helper who didn't steal Christmas but stole our hearts instead. If you guessed the Grinch, you're absolutely right.

A woman drove up just minutes after, her trunk filled with new toys. She was smiling, as was her son in his car seat. The little boy was autistic. She explained in Shel's ear that the Grinch is his favorite. Of course, Shel repeated this in the Grinch's ear.

The Grinch jumped down and joined the little fan in the back seat to say hi and merry Christmas, as we wiped tears from our eyes.

We witness the power of God throughout the years, as I've said previously. God has Shel's attention. I'm sure we make Him smile and laugh (especially seeing Shel ride a bike around the warehouse or scaring us with her snakes).

I never planned to be an elf, yet I'm convinced I was meant to run into this crazy lady with a goal to reach thousands of children near and far. We've helped towns ravaged by tornados and floods and traveled to South Dakota to an Indian School, Saint Jude, and Boys Town with supplies. We help homeless vets and provide for local army reserve units at Christmas for their children. As Shel says, "We're a force of goodness in this world."

The next chapter, "Angels among Us," honors more unsung heroes, our local friends, past and present. Ever faithful, they are truly "the wind beneath our wings."

Santa and Friends.

Christian.

FOR THE LOVE
OF CHILDREN IS WHY
WE ARE HERE

LOONEY TUNES
That's all
EXIT
Folks

Chapter 9

ANGELS AMONG US

Our circle of angels grows with each year, like an ever-widening ring from a stone tossed in the water.

Orland Park, Illinois, is located twenty-six miles southwest of Chicago, with a population of fifty-one thousand. We salute the police and fire departments for their continued friendship. Every year the fire department conducts a toy drive from each fire station at Christmas. New toys are collected and delivered to the warehouse. We are so fortunate to be part of this community. Parents arrive with their children to deliver new toys. I'll always remember the young couple carrying a newborn, explaining they are beginning a holiday tradition of donating to those less fortunate in the hope to instill the joy in giving back to their child. We have a wonderful group who organizes a toy drive in their subdivision. Many families collect new and used toys from their neighborhoods, load up their vans, and deliver them to our warehouse. I'll always remember the mom who struggled carrying a hobbyhorse through the door. Many of you might not remember the huge horse often seen in businesses. Kids loved getting on and playing cowboy, rocking back and forth. It seems the woman told her son, "If you don't let me donate this thing, I'm bringing it to your dorm room!" We love receiving books and bikes, puzzles and games, and larger items too. Play kitchens and dollhouses are often recycled to community centers for endless enjoyment.

WGN, our television station, featured Toybox on their morning show. Our donations increased beyond Orland Park to include Chicago and suburbs, near and far.

We also love the idea a mom had to make small blankets for Beanie Babies for children to hold and cuddle, including a note in each gift. So many have become angels. All contribute to our mission to reach more and more children with every year. Our sincere thanks to all of you.

We have elves who spread Christmas cheer by distributing small toys we provide. Mary has become a dear friend who drives through her Chicago neighborhood stopping at laundromats, delighting children with her warmth and gift of a matchbox car or little doll. A barber gives toys to kids coming in at Christmas, and there's Tommy, who organizes a coat drive every year and delivers them to the homeless. Tommy is a marine who drives to areas in the country experiencing hardship, delivering much-needed items of clothing or household necessities. Bill, together with his friends, is always ready to help. Al is our bike man who, in retirement, has repaired over six thousand bicycles. Rich and Anita Hallman, the Passero family and volunteers from DuPage Toys for Tots, thank you! We appreciate all of you and also those who contribute a gift card or cash. We are humbled by your generosity and so very honored to call you friends.

Our loyal businesses year in and year out have proven their dedication to the community they serve. We would be remiss not to mention Marquette Bank volunteers who help at our fundraisers or whenever they are called on. Kohl's volunteers come from Orland Park and other stores when needed. We receive books from Barnes & Noble at Christmas and a wonderful holiday luncheon from Giordano's Pizza. Costco; Home Depot; Lowes; Ron from Megent Financial who, together with his family, decorates and donates wreaths every Christmas; Meijer Foods; Beggars Pizza; Durbins'; Ed and Joe's Restaurant; Giordano's; PetSmart; the Tow Truck for Tots drivers for their truck parade and toy donations; Fritz Nothnagel; Capri Restaurant in Palos Heights, Illinois, for their annual toy drive; and the Andrew Foundation are loyal contributors. We salute you!

Until recently, all we had was a manual pallet jack. A most welcome donation was the gift of a power jack from Midway Industrial Equipment. Thanks so much.

One day, a woman came in with toys, and Shel, as she often does, went on and on about Toybox Connection. The woman, moved to tears, went home and relayed all she heard that day. Well, what wonderful loyal friends Lynn and Frank have become. Frank is president of the IUEC, the International Union of Elevator Constructors. Thank you and the IUEC for all you do every year to help our goal of reaching more children. Thanks to all the unions we have been blessed to meet with Frank's help.

Lastly, thanks to our volunteers past and present. Special mention to Richard Parker, Lee, and Bob Zychowski, three of our angels who now are angels in heaven. Volunteers are unpaid but receive much more than a paycheck. We all feel we were meant to come together and truly love what we do. Thanks to our husbands who are constantly called upon to repair items, inflate balls, add batteries, make deliveries and who do not complain when we're too tired to make dinner. Thanks to Shel's family and mine for their help and support. You're the best.

No matter who you are, everyone has the opportunity to
be an angel. Anytime you give of yourself, your time, your
talent, and your resources to help another human being,
you can consider yourself in the Company of Angels.
—Michelle Maxia

The Annual Tow Trucks for Tots Day.

Chapter 10

THE GIVING TREE

Dear readers, indulge yourselves. Take a few minutes to reflect on what Christmas was like when you were a child. Reminisce about the department store windows, the streetlights adorned with wreaths and bows, the huge Christmas tree downtown, and a trip to visit the big man himself, sit on his knee, and stammer your wish list. Remember the letter to the North Pole after checking out the latest and greatest toys in the catalogs and the decorations? Did you have reindeer tracks in the snow when you bounded out of bed and ran to your parents' room to jump on them, anxious to see what the jolly old elf brought? Do you recall your parents decking the halls? The dozens of cookies, the gifts, the traditions, the comforts of a home filled with joy? My mom saved tinsel. Each strand was placed on the branch (when she wasn't looking, I tossed it on).

For the poor, the holidays are exasperating. They underscore the effects of struggling to provide basic necessities after working two or three jobs.

The Giving Tree began as a sapling in Michelle Maxia's garage. Its branches grew strong and became interwoven, bending but never breaking. Each nonprofit is a branch that receives nourishment from the roots, which anchor our tree and keep it healthy. You are the roots; without you we would wither and fall.

We were contacted by our local television station, WGN, who featured us on their news. We have been fortunate to be featured in

51

newspapers, which also brought nonprofits to our door. Year after year we help one another. We provide toys for a burn camp, cancer camp, and foster kids' camp. A tree of sharing for all seasons.

Michelle told of some of her experiences, relating, "I cannot possibly list all the nonprofits on our tree, but will share a few branches. One day, just before Christmas when we were still at the warehouse, a woman called. She said she had just left an abusive relationship and was asking for help in providing toys for her little girl. I explained that we don't provide toys for individuals but work with nonprofits. The woman was about to hang up when I said, 'Wait, I can give you names and telephone numbers of organizations we work with. They can help you.' A few days after Christmas, the woman called again to say she couldn't thank me enough. The organization I connected her with helped her with rent and food. If everyone called needing help, I would spend days verifying their qualifications. I connect people with other nonprofits who can give so much more than toys.

"I was at the warehouse another day when a mom came in who had two boys about eleven and twelve. She mentioned she wanted to adopt a child. I told her about the Hephzibah Home for children in Oak Park, Illinois. About six months went by, and she came back with a donation of girls' toys. I remembered she had boys and asked her what she was doing with girls' toys. She explained she contacted the Hephzibah Home and adopted a little girl. Never did I imagine I would be a part of giving a child a home. That was a very big branch. If Toybox went away tomorrow, I would know this single connection was worth it all.

"Together with K-Love radio, we brought toys to the Ronald McDonald House the day before Christmas Eve." Ronald McDonald provides lodging and meals for families when their children are hospitalized. We were given the names and ages of the kids. Their gifts were age appropriate, and each present included one of their names on them, which made them personal. "They were so surprised Santa found them!"

Early nonprofits on our tree included ACT Coalition and Englewood Safety Net in Chicago, Alicia's House, Together We Cope, American Indian Center, Clara's House, Easterseals, Grant

A Wish, Operation Homefront, Helmet to Hardhats, My Joyful Heart, Shepherd's House, Bridge Teen Center, St. Jude, Easterseals Crisis Center, and several schools in low-income areas. Later, Camp Quality, Camp "I Am Me," Camp Royalty, and Blessed Child came aboard. Ira and his nonprofit, Illinois Partners In Hope, unceasingly work with us to provide assistance near and far. The list is endless.

As volunteers, we pay attention, along with Shel's family and friends to local news, on the chance we learn of an opportunity to help other nonprofits. As the boss always says, "Need has no season."

Michelle
Jacob Makena Mike

A COVID Christmas.

Chapter 11

THE POWER OF FAITH

In *Man's Search for Meaning* by psychiatrist and Holocaust survivor Viktor Frankl, he explains the purpose of life: purposeful work, love, and courage in the face of difficultly. When we have purpose we move beyond the day-to-day monotony born of routine. Without purpose, we welcome our problems and entertain them with negativity. We are all guilty of self-absorption.

My purpose in writing this book is to inspire you. Reach out in your community. Collect gently used toys and clothing and bring them to homeless shelters. Bring used books and playground equipment to schools in lower income areas. Turn on your "heart lights," and your own troubles will diminish. In the words of Dr. Martin Luther King Jr., "You don't have to see the whole staircase, just take the first step."

Shel explains, "For the first time in my life, I felt hope. Having hope launched my belief that I had faith and that faith could grow. I kept a notepad and pen on a table next to my bed at night to write my thought so I wouldn't forget. I was praying one night and asking about faith and a quiet voice came to me and said, "**F**aith is feeling **as if t**here's **h**ope—**FAITH**."

Shel is the catalyst that was given power through faith to begin her dream, a dream that is shared and instills hope in others. We receive countless letters of thanks, but truly we are thankful to spread joy to those less fortunate.

Michelle's story needed to be told. It is a heartfelt journey of discovery. If we are fortunate to be published, all proceeds will be donated to Toybox Connection to continue our goal of being "a moving force of goodness in the world."

Appendix

Dear friend,

Thank you for the awesome board games. I really like paying Monopoly and connect 4. It is so much fun!

love,
Janiah

Dear Michelle,

Thank you very much for donating all the wonderful items to me. It has been a difficult time for me to gather enough money for necessities for my baby When my case manager and her coworker arrived at my door with all this stuff, I felt like I was receiving gifts on Christmas. It was very generous to give this many items to one individual. Luckily my nursery room can hold it all. I am very blessed to have this many items stocked up for my baby. The formula boxes will be helpful for backup. My baby will love the colorful bouncer later on. My favorite item was the new bed in memory foam format. Now, I finally have my own comfortable bed. The fragrance set is perfect since I love perfumes. I am very pleased with your charity and grateful to be a recipient of your gifts. I appreciate you and all you do. Sincerely, Bryttor

Michelle Maxia,
Toy Box Connection
PO Box 1146
Orland Park, IL 60462

Dear Michelle,

On behalf of Mooseheart Child City & School, I want to take this moment to say thank you and offer our gratitude for your continual donations to Mooseheart!

On Monday May 17th, 2021 Toy Box Connection played a key role in our Community Gathering. You all provided a taco truck, chips and water for our entire campus (250 people). Furthermore, desserts prepared for all of our homes and youth to enjoy! In addition, having you all on campus for a tour was a celebrated time. Now you can see what you do day in day out makes a direct and immediate impact to our youth and staff.

We are so appreciative of Toy Box Connection!! Mooseheart is ever so delighted to be a part of the ripple effects that you make in the Community! Thank you once again for taking the time to come to Mooseheart for a tour, the taco truck, food and drinks!! You truly increased the fun and dynamics of our Community Gathering.

Mooseheart is proud to be a part of the Toy Box Connection Family for so many years since 2009, but who's counting? ☺

630-723-2092

Mooseheart Child City & Sc
255 James J. Davis Dr.

Bryan Miller
Dean of Students/Behavior Interventionist
Head Coach High School Girls Basketball
630-723-2092

Mooseheart Child City & School Inc.
255 James J. Davis Dr.
Mooseheart, IL 60539
www.mooseheart.org

Camp Quality Family,

At our 23rd week of Camp Quality Illinois, our campers and volunteers traveled through five different eras in our week themed, "Camp Quality Travels Through Time." During a week of the most beautiful weather we have likely ever had at Camp Quality, and rain drop totals that I could count on my own two hands, we visited Prehistoric Times, Ancient Greece, Ancient Rome, The Wild West, and Renaissance.

Campers danced, participated in daily scavenger hunts, went on motor-cycle rides, hummer rides, army truck rides, and antique car rides. They got to spend time at the pool, the craft room, archery and paintball. They jumped in inflatables, played gaga ball and basketball, watched mov-ies and played board games. Most importantly they made a week full of memories and friends that will last a lifetime.

None of this would be possible without the generosity of our donors and the dedication of our volunteers. We are able to provide a unique one-on-one experience to our campers because there are well over one hundred people out there willing to give so generously of their time.

We also have an extremely dedicated Camp Organizing Committee, for which I am extremely thankful. We are saying "see you soon!" to a few members who are retiring from our COC this year, but we know aren't really going to be far away. In fact, we will probably see all of them at camp in some capacity next year! While I'm thankful for each and every one of my COC members, from those who have been around since camp started in 1995 to those who decided to take the plunge and step into a new role for 2018, I would like to extend an extra special thank you to Bud, Carol, and LeAnn for their many years of dedication and service to Camp Quality and support of me as director as they retire this year.

Whether a parent, a camper, a volunteer, or a donor, I hope that as you look through the pages of this book, you're able to see the positive impact each of us has on those around us. While our number one priority is the safety and happiness of our campers, so much more comes from being a part of something so special.

I am blessed to call you all my Camp Quality Family. Thank you for being a part of something so special!

Sincerely,
Mary ___

About the Author

Diane L. O'Brien is a deeply religious woman of faith and a loving wife, mother, and grandmother.

After working several years for the telephone company, she has dedicated her retirement to helping those less fortunate through her volunteer work at Toybox Connection, a Chicago area nonprofit.